Sacrifices

Sacrifices

TITHES AND OFFERINGS

Averil Burke-St. Marthe

© 2017 Averil Burke-St. Marthe
All rights reserved.

ISBN: 1548650455
ISBN 13: 9781548650452

Table of Contents

My Story · vii

Chapter 1 Tithes and Offerings · 1
    What are Tithes and what are Offerings? · · · · · · · · · · · 1
    Order · 4
    Seed · 6
    Sowing · 8
    The Mind · 10
    Character · 12

Chapter 2 The Supernatural and the Anointing · · · · · · · 15
    The Bible · 15
    Words · 17
    Spirit · 19
    The Blood · 22

Chapter 3 Blockage to the Flow of God · · · · · · · · · · · · · 25
    Habit · 25
    Addiction · 27
    Struggles · 29
    Weakness/Weariness · 31
    Obstruction · 33
    Hindrance · 35
    Limits · 37

Chapter 4 Manifestation and Power of the Living God 40
                Changes 40
                Values 42
                Quality 44
                Success 46
Chapter 5 Impossibility Made Possible 50
                Loyalty 50
                Hope 52
                God Got This 55

                Conclusion 59
                Scripture References 61
                Acknowledgment 65
                Bibliography 67

My Story

My name is Averil Burke-St. Marthe, and this is my story. I am a very active and involved member of my church, New Vision of Hope, and I have always paid my tithes and given my offerings generously and cheerfully. I am well respected, and people label me as not in need of anything because I appear to have everything. I am also a very creative and talented person and can do quite a number of things to help myself.

What people could not see was how alone I felt. I was surrounded by people but was still alone.

Life has dealt me some hard blows. For example, the deaths of my grandmother, my mother, and my uncle. These people I loved dearly, and when they were alive, they were like my anchor. Death took them away from me. To add to that pressure, I had to leave my son behind when I came to the United States with my daughter to live with my husband. I was in a new and strange place starting a new life. My daughter has matured since then and is now living independently in her own apartment.

Three years ago, my husband was diagnosed with rectal cancer, and he went through vigorous treatments and operations. Thank God, he survived all those treatments, and he is alive. As if that was not enough, I was involved in an accident, and I too went through surgery. Not knowing how to open up to people, I kept my inner feelings buckled up inside. I engaged in what gave me pleasure and what gave me joy and a sense of security. I did not want to feel vulnerable to people. I began shopping excessively. I became a shopaholic.

Although I enjoyed shopping, it caused me grief and pain. I was now facing credit-card debt that was climbing along with my everyday obligations and expenses. Guilt set in. I no longer was able to pay tithes and offerings, and I chose to pay my bills, which to me were more urgent. I felt and I knew in my spirit that this was wrong.

One Sunday, I went to church and could not stop crying. I felt guilty and ashamed. I got up out of my seat in church and went up to the altar, confessed to my pastor and the congregation what I had done. I asked God for His forgiveness because I had been robbing Him, God, of my tithes and offerings, which were needed in the church so God's work could continue. I repented there at the altar.

My life has never been the same since that time. In fact, God is now using my test and has given me a testimony. He has taken my weakness and mess and used it and myself to teach others about tithes and offerings. The apostles had me talk at my church on tithes and offerings. At the end of this talk, I proclaimed in my conclusion when I was informed by them that I would be back, teaching on this same very topic. But in my mind, I had said it all, and I was at the end of this presentation. I did not know anything more to say on this topic. My daughter said to me, if they, the apostles, say you have more to say, then God has more for you to say. She said, "Go to God and ask Him what He wants you to say."

I went home, sat in my bathroom, looked up to heaven, and said to God, "God, I do not know what else to say on tithes and offerings. God, if you want me to continue speaking on this topic, you will have to tell me what to say because at this very moment, I am at a loss, and my mind is totally blank."

As I sat there in my bathroom looking up at the ceiling to heaven, through my spiritual eyes, I saw a pair of hands with the palms held in an upward position, as if receiving or giving something. It started to float down toward me and stopped over my head. The hand opened, and whatever was in the hand fell on my head. Instantly, the scales came off my eyes, and I saw as if the world opened up, and different topics started floating around me. I screamed out loudly, *"Wow, wow,"* as this picture and those words entered into my mind.

Not only were these topics given to me, but also God took me on a different journey or route like no other: how to explain about tithes and offerings. The presentations were to demonstrate the uniqueness and awesomeness of the Creator God. They were to be presented in such a way as to show the order in which God wants us to give or present our gifts to Him. They were to capture, cultivate, and demonstrate how powerful it is to give and how happy we are when we receive.

God used me to explain the purpose of tithes and offerings. God also showed me how to get out of debt, while using me to teach others, and at the same time how to get out of this mess I gotten myself into. God has not stopped there. He has now elevated me to another level, and you are a witness to it through the writing of this book on tithes and offerings. God wants us to know that He is a God of order. As it is in the natural, so it is in the spiritual. As it was back then in biblical times, so it is now. In fact, it runs parallel. We are spiritual beings living in a natural world and experiencing natural feelings. However, to achieve the spiritual, you have to line up in the natural.

There are rules, regulations, and laws in the natural world that you have to live by and obey. In the spiritual world, you have rules, laws, and regulations that you have to abide by also, but you have something more: faith. When you have faith anchored to God, you cannot go wrong. God will pick you up when you fall and carry you when you are weak. He said to put your trust in Him. Faith is what will carry you through in tough times. Faith is what you believe in. It is things hoped for but not seen. This is a spiritual connection with God—your faith. Faith will never fail.

This book shows that God is our main source and supplier. With God, all things are possible. After all, we are His creation, and He loves us unconditionally. If only we knew the plans God had for us at creation when He created us and the plans He has for us now—for us to succeed even though we are so sinful and a stiff-necked set of people. That is why God sent His Son, Jesus, to die on the Cross for our sins so that we can be redeemed back to Him. He wants us to be successful and succeed in every area in our lives here on earth as well as to reign with Him in Heaven when we die. So be of good courage and be blessed.

After reading my book, I am positive you will be able to get a glimpse of the grandeur and awesomeness of God. You will realize that no matter how powerful and great or how rich you think you are, this book will allow you to see how fragile, vulnerable, and susceptible a person is to the many changes that take place in a person's life as well as the many challenges that person will have to face from day to day. We sometimes end up doing the opposite of what we originally set out to do, or we get sidetracked from the goals we had planned.

This book will demonstrate the power of giving and the power of receiving. A hand that is closed and tight fisted will never be able to give freely and likewise will not receive freely. As we stretch our hands out to give, the hand is already open and in a position to receive.

Last but not least, this book will give you hope. God created us. We are His masterpiece. God said that the hairs on our heads are numbered and that He knows how many hairs are on each of our heads as individuals. When He finished creating us, He looked at His creation, blew His breath into us, and declared this was indeed good. We have our children, but we will never know those intricate details about them, but our God knows. That shows us and expresses to us how much God cares for us and how much He loves us. He went a step further and died on the Cross for all our sins. That by itself speaks volumes. Would you do that?

The people of the world are taking biblical principles, applying them to their lives, and enjoying success. Example of this is, some people in business have made allowances in their businesses to give to charity, education and research. One research facility, St. Jude Hospital, caters to cancer children and their families. This hospital provides vital education programs to the next generation of cancer specialists. Families of cancer patients never receive a bill from St. Jude's hospital for treatment, travel, housing or food. The business place on-the-other hand receives a tax cut benefit which becomes beneficial to them. This will move God's hand to bless and prosper their business. As you give to God's people, He will multiply His giving back to you.

Why can't we as Christians, who are anchored in the Lord, do the same—do what is right and what we are supposed to do, especially in the church? When we follow God's directions, this allows more souls to come into the Kingdom, be saved, and be delivered. When we apply biblical principles and follow God's teachings and instructions, there is no way God will not keep His promises to us. There is no way He will not come see about us.

This book will definitely show the proper way to offer sacrifices, especially your tithes and offerings, your time, and your talent. This shows that there are many benefits and many blessings in being obedient and following God's Word and His instructions. Since making this change, one of the blessings I have had is God taking me out of credit-card debts. I have also acquired a new vehicle, a Lexus NX200t. I have a different approach and respect to life, people, and things I meet. God will hold us accountable. Some people will never go to a church. They, however, will observe our lives and look to us as leaders for direction. If we continue to do the wrong things, then we will lead astray others who are looking to us for directions. My encounter with God and this book has changed my life for the better, and I am sure it will do the same for you.

CHAPTER 1
Tithes and Offerings

WHAT ARE TITHES AND WHAT ARE OFFERINGS?

TITHES ARE 10 PERCENT OF your **talent,** 10 percent of your **time,** and 10 percent of your **gross income.** Gross income is income before any deductions. Net income is income after all deductions are taken out from the gross income. Offerings are a freewill offering where you decide the amount you want to give. This is in addition to your tithes. How much you give as offerings demonstrates the personal relationship you have with Almighty God. The Bible states that when giving, it should be done joyfully and willingly, not grudgingly. When given as God says and the way He says we are to present it, it is now a sacrifice given to God without blemish or wrinkles and is spotless. It is also a sweet smell to God's nostrils.

What is God's purpose for our tithes? God's purpose for our tithes is very clear. Malachi 3:10 says, "Bring ye all the tithes into the storehouse, that there be meat in mine house." In the biblical days, God selected the Levites and the priest to carry out His work in His house only, and these specially assigned people could do nothing else. They could not work the land or do anything outside of working in the tabernacle. These people had families, so God made sure that these people, the Levi, priest, and their families, could survive, live, and have food. God did not want them to have to worry about how to maintain their families. The tithes were for that purpose. God required the children of Israel to give to the Levites and priest from all their possessions, 10 percent of the very best, as tithes. The offering, the extra that they decided how much to give, was used for the upkeep of the tabernacle. In our time, the freewill offering is used for the upkeep and maintenance of our church buildings, e.g. rent, mortgage, light, telephone, salary for workers, etc. It is also for the work of God in the world at large and also carrying out missionary work. God also made provisions for the orphans and widows in biblical times but it also applies to present times as well. These sets of people had no family, so the church helped to take care of them.

Today, our modern-day Levite is pastor or leader of the church, whom God has placed in each vineyard to shepherd us, to oversee us, and to teach and direct us into all Truth and God's Word. He is there also to pray for us to be healed of our sicknesses and diseases, and a lot of us have been healed. Not to mention that when a person accepts Christ as their Lord and Savior, he or she becomes covered under the Blood, and they now have a Blood-covering relationship with Christ. He or she has the church, which now becomes his or her spiritual home, where he or she will be spiritually fed with the Word. God promised that He would withhold nothing good from us.

God did not plan for there to be any lack in His house. If every member of the Body of Christ were faithful in giving his or her tithes and offerings to the church, there would be more than enough with which to fulfill the work of God around the world. We would have the necessary finances to evangelize the entire world and bring in the final harvest of souls before Christ's return.

Deuteronomy 12:5–6 states, "But unto the place which the Lord your God shall choose out of your tribes to put His name there, even unto his habitation shall ye seek, and thither thou shall ye seek, and thither thou shall bring your burnt offering, and your sacrifices, and your tithes and heave offerings of your hand, and your vows, and your freewill offerings, and the firstlings of your herds and of your flocks."

The local church is the storehouse and is only a small part of God's storehouse. God holds individuals responsible for distribution of the tithes and offerings. When individuals obeyed God fully with their tithes and offerings, they are able to go directly to God and ask God's supernatural blessings be released upon them. When you act in obedience to God, it sets in motion a chain of events that causes God's promises to happen. Where the Word of God is preached, there is a demonstration of **power,** where souls are continually being won into the Kingdom of God and where people are healed and delivered by the miracle-working power of God. Unlimited, liberal giving by you, the people, will result in unlimited, liberal giving by God.

When we withhold or fail to give God our tithes, we are robbing God. We are stealing from God what rightfully belongs to Him. God asked in Malachi 3:8–9, "Will a man rob God? Yet ye have robbed me. But ye say, wherein have we robbed thee? In tithes and offerings. Ye are cursed with a curse: for ye have robbed me, even this whole nation."

So today, let us stop robbing God. Let us repent for withholding our tithes and offerings and let us confess our sins to God and ask Him for His forgiveness. God's Word teaches us in Proverbs 3:9–10, "Honor the Lord with thy substances, and with the first fruits of all thine increases: so shall thy barns be filled with plenty, and thy presses shall burst out with new wines."

Many live in financial bondage because they have not been faithful and obedient in giving God their tithes. God is saying to the church, as He said to the children of Israel, in Malachi 3:7, "Return unto me, and I will return unto you, said the Lord of Host."

As you take this step of faith today, believe that God will break the bondage of debt from your life, open the windows of heaven, and pour out His supernatural increases upon you until there will not be enough room to receive it.

ORDER
Order (N)

- An authoritative direction or instruction; command; mandate
- A condition in which each thing is properly disposed with reference to other things and its purpose; methodical or harmonious arrangement
- Proper, satisfactory, or working condition
- Conformity or obedience to law or established authority; absence of disturbance, riot, revolt, unruliness
- Prevailing course or arrangement of things; established system or regime

God is a man of excellence and order, and He wants His people to act and live in excellence and have an abundant life. That is why He is bringing the church back to basics.

He is doing the same thing with us in New Vision of Hope as He did with Moses and the Israelites, whom He had as His chosen people. My only hope is that we do not take forty years to get it right when it could be done in eleven days. He had the children of Israel in the desert for forty years, teaching them the right way to carry out the task and the proper way to present their gifts to Him. This was an eleven-day journey under normal circumstances. He showed them there was a blessing in doing the right thing, and there were consequences when things were done the wrong way.

We find that God is a current God. In biblical times, the people traded using animals, food, and even people. A lamb, dove, or calf without blemish was used for the atonement of our sins. The blood had to be shed and sprinkled at the altar. A special person assigned by God, called priest or Levi, had to perform these duties on behalf of the people to God for forgiveness of their sins. These special people, the Levi and priests, had to be sanctified before they could perform these duties.

However, when Jesus came on the scene, He became that sacrificial lamb when He died on the cross and His Blood was shed for all our sins.

He became sin who committed no sin. No longer do we have to shed animal blood for our sins. No longer do we use food, animals, or people to trade. We use money as our currency. Therefore, Jesus became that bridge between then (the biblical times) and now (current times). We can now go straight to God, talk to God, ask for His forgiveness of our sins, and know that He hears us and forgives us. We read about the miracle back then in the Bible, and we have seen the miracles happening now, especially in our midst here in the church and in the world.

We are a natural being living in a natural world with a spiritual soul. This being said, although we are spiritual beings, we are living in a natural world and having natural experiences. As it is in the natural, so it is in the spiritual. We need order in everything we do in both the natural as well as the spiritual. One of the things God emphasizes in the Bible is that we are to respect those in authority who are placed over us. We might not like the person, but we must respect the title.

When Jesus was asked by the authorities if He and His men should pay taxes, He simply said to Peter to go down to the sea and look at what he found in the first fish's mouth. Peter found a coin, and Jesus asked him whose picture was on the coin. Peter said Caesar. Jesus then said, give to Cesar what belongs to Caesar and give to God what belongs to God.

Here, apostles, priests, and bishops are carrying out the will of God by instructing us, the people, in what God is informing them that He wants us as a church body to do within the church and our everyday lives. This will allow us to operate in excellence. Things will go smoothly, and there will be no confusion(s), especially among His people. If we are called upon in the natural by those in authority, our books and the church will be in order. In the spiritual, when God appears to the body of Christ, we will be ready. We will not be a hindrance to those who desire to come into the church, and just like us, they can come in, be saved, and accept Christ as their savior, be delivered, healed, and set free.

The same thing with tithes and offerings. These gifts are holy to God. God wants us to present our gifts in a particular way. That is cheerfully and joyfully. A specified amount is stated, which is 10 percent of our gross income, as tithes for the caring of our minister(s) and a freewill offering of our choice amount for the maintenance of the church, where the needs of God's house will be supplied and met.

When we do this, God promises to pour out a blessing, and we will not have enough room to store it. So, do what is right, which is paying our tithes and offerings.

Isaiah 55:11 says, "So shall my word be that goeth forth out of my mouth: it shall not return unto me void, but it shall accomplish that which I please, and it shall prosper in the thing whereto I sent it."

Seed
Seed (N)

- The fertilized, matured ovule of a flowering plant, containing an embryo or rudimentary plant
- Any propagative part of a plant, including tubers, bulb, etc., especially as preserved for growing a new crop
- Any similar small part or fruit
- Offspring
- Sperm; semen
- To place, introduce, etc., especially in the hope of increase or profit

Proverbs 3: 9–10 says, "Honor the Lord with thy substance, and with the first fruit of all thine increases: So shall thy barns be filled with plenty, and thy presses shall burst out with new wine."

Regardless of the circumstances that we may be facing right now, God is saying to us, "Put Me first! Trust Me, and My promise to you! Test Me and prove Me! I will be faithful in opening the windows of blessings and my abundance to you!" God is saying to you, "I am bound to you by my Word. You will receive all that I have promised, an excess of good things to enjoy when you remain faithful and obedient to Me."

It is essential for you to understand why the tithe was so important to God and why your tithe is so important today. God does not need our money. All the wealth in this world is His. Haggai 2:8 states "The silver is mine, and the gold is mine, saith the Lord of hosts." God wants us to give our tithes because it recognizes and honors Him, the source of our supply. God wants to use our tithes as a means to meet our needs, but they all belong to Him. This is called sowing a seed.

Our beloved apostle, Apostle Cassandra who was a coleader of New Vision of Hope Ministry, God rest her soul, sowed her seed, not only to God and her family, but she sowed a seed in all of us. We saw how she selflessly worked for God regardless of how sick she felt. She was at church every Sunday pouring into us what God told and gave her to impart to us and in us. We will see a manifestation and impartation not only in our generation but also in generations to come based on what was taught to us by her. We do not understand why God took her now, but one thing we do understand is that God's work must go on. That is what she stood for and believed. She would be glad to know that we are carrying on God's work in this ministry. To honor God and show our appreciation to her and Apostle Scotto White in this ministry, we have to do our part by paying our tithes and our freewill offerings. This will ensure that our doors will remain open and our bills are paid.

In the days of Moses, the Israelites were fighting, and Moses's arms became tired, and they were kept up by his two armor bearers. As long as his arms were up, they were winning the fight, but when he could not keep them up and his arms came down, they started to lose the fight. His armor bearers came forward and helped to keep his arms up until they won the fight. This is one of the ways in which us saints in New Vision of Hope can keep our apostle's arms up: by doing the right thing, which is paying our tithes and offerings and whatever else is required of us and by not holding back.

Let us, therefore, sow some seeds today, seeds of our tithes and offerings, so that the ministry's doors can stay open and the bills can be met. Seeds of love, encouragement, and loyalty to the ministry, especially in the form of our attendance, help us watch its growth. The pastors and ministers have a lot on their minds along with the weight of the ministry carried on their shoulders. Along with that come the various personalities of their members that they have to deal with. Let us not add to their worries. Remember, we have to take care of our pastors and ministers as best as we can.

Therefore, let us sow our best seeds and watch what God will do in and to the ministry and to each person individually and collectively.

Sow your seed.

Sowing
Sowing (V)

- To scatter seed over (land, earth, etc.) for their purpose of growth
- To sow seed, as for the production of a crop

A planter decides on the crop he or she wants to invest in. He or she gets all the ingredients together that are needed. If it is a field—the plot of land, location, the seeds, the necessary people/workers to help in the process, good soil, water, and fertilization. The tools—e.g., fork, oxen as in the biblical days to plow the land, sprinklers, and all other various equipment necessary for the job, which will depend on how sophisticated you want your process to be.

After the land is prepared, the seed is then planted. Depending on the type of seeds or plant, you might have to diligently monitor and patiently upkeep the crop until time for harvest. During this period, you have to wait, and while waiting, you have an expectation that with all the groundwork you have done, it will pay off with the manifestation of a good crop and a good harvest. You have an expectation that you will be able to harvest a full crop and that everything will be all right; you will be able to make a profit and have a market for your product. You know that you did all the groundwork necessary that was in your power and control and that you did it right. That is more reason for you to expect good returns on your investment.

The same thing applies with the workplace. You applied for a job, went on the interview, were successful, and got the job. They promised you that at the end of a specified period, you would be paid a certain amount. You accepted the job based on those promises and went forth willingly and joyfully to do the job with the expectation of getting paid. You had high expectations and faith that they would honor their word; in other words, they would fulfill the promise. They would honor what was agreed upon in the interview. In the end, you would reap the harvest that you sowed. If you were a good worker, they would retain you, but if you were a bad worker, you would be fired.

Well, the same thing that applies in the natural also applies in the spiritual. In the Bible, God said if you paid your tithes of 10 percent and a freewill offering, He would pour out so many blessings that you would not have room enough to receive them all. God is telling us to have an expectation, especially when you do something in His Kingdom. When you freely do these things in the ministry, let God be your focus and not a person. Do the things not to get praised but to enhance the Kingdom of God. In doing this, you allow the church doors to remain open, bills are met, souls that come into the Kingdom are saved and delivered, and the Levi (priest/ministers) is taken care of.

God is saying if you do your part, have faith in Him, show love to each other, have an expectation, do right, and live right, He will withhold nothing from His people. Be Christ-like in all you do.

A seed is just a seed until planted or sowed. It is only after a seed is planted that it will and can germinate into a harvest. When you release the seed from your hand, you draw God's attention, and this action is what allows God to start acting on your behalf.

In conclusion, sow seeds into the Kingdom of God and expect a harvest from God.

The Mind
Mind (N)

- In human or other conscious being, the element, part, substance, or process that reasons, thinks, feels, wills, perceives, judges, etc.: the processes of the human mind.
- The totality of conscious and unconscious mental processes and activities.
- Intellect or understanding, as distinguished from the faculties of feeling and willing; intelligence

The mind is a very powerful thing, mass, substance, or matter—however you want to label it. A statement says whatever the mind conceives, it can and will achieve. Firstly, we have to understand who we are. We are offspring from the Creator, who is God Almighty. He is also the creator of this world. He spoke the world into existence. He made us in His image and blew His breath into us. Naturally, we are going to be creative human beings.

One example of this creativity can be seen in the Bible with the children of Babel. These people were of one accord and decided to build a structure from earth to heaven. They would have accomplished this task had God not intervened and made each person start speaking in a different language, thus causing confusion. They were no longer able to communicate with each other.

Another person was David. From an early age as a child, he was sent out all by himself to tend to the sheep. He had to become creative in defending himself and his sheep from the deer, bears, and wolves. We saw how he developed his skill in defending himself and his sheep to the point where he used these same precise skills to defeat Goliath, the Philistine's giant, who had everyone afraid of him.

In our midst is my daughter Anna-Kay, who is a praise dancer, and Prophetess Margaret, who is a praise mime. They use these forms of art or technique to portray a character, mood, idea, or narration by gesture and bodily movements that spring from the mind. The mind conceptualizes, and the body actualizes; we, being of the same accord, can visualize, interpret, and make perceptible to the mind or imagination an understanding of what we have seen. The amazing thing is that one person can minister to an audience of thousands of people using the mind, facial expressions, gesticulations of the limbs, and the movement of the body, while not uttering a word, to portray a message that can be received by all. This is how powerful the mind is.

God is saying the same thing to us spiritually. He is saying that when we accept Christ as our Savior, we become spiritually connected and covered under His Blood. As a result, as we read and hear His Words, it builds up our faith. When we can see and receive what we have heard or read spiritually and accept it mentally, then there will be an outward demonstration physically. It is all in the mind. The power of the mind.

God is the power source and Creator for all humankind whether we accept Him or not. For those of us who accept Him and because we have a divine connection with Him, He promises to open the windows of heaven and pour out so many blessings, healing, and deliverance to us that we will not have room enough to receive and store it all. We have to visualize it mentally first, and then we will be able to accept it by faith.

However, there are a few other things God requires and requests of us. He said for us to have faith and believe. Matthew 21:22 says, "And all things, whatsoever ye shall ask in prayer, believing, ye shall receive." Even if our faith is as small as a mustard seed, we can speak to our mountain and say, "Be thou removed," and it will be done. God said He gives us power to stomp on the devil's head that is under our feet. God also said to give so that His house will have meat to meet the needs of His people and His house. Souls can come into His Kingdom, and they can be saved, be delivered, and be set free. God said to give 10 percent of our time, 10 percent of our talent, and 10 percent of our income as tithes so His work can continue. God also tells us to give freely and joyfully, not grudgingly, a freewill offering to meet expenses. Do this in faith and see the miracles that will follow.

We move by faith and not sight. This is how powerful the mind is and can be. Whatever you can believe, God will allow to happen. And what is done in secret, the manifestation of God's blessings will be seen openly.

CHARACTER
Character (N)

- The aggregate of features and traits that form the individual nature of some people
- Qualities of honesty, courage, or the like
- A person, especially with reference to behavior or personality

As little kids, when asked what they would like to be when they grow up, they have no problem in dreaming big. This is because they are pure, coming from God, and they have not been exposed or contaminated by the world or labeled by the people they meet. As they become exposed to these people, i.e., the family, the community, schools, friends, and coworkers, their focus becomes tainted. People start labeling them, and limitations start to become a reality. Their capabilities and capacity to do and be are no longer there, and they start to adapt and act the way people say they are. Sometimes they even start to compare themselves to others, and jealousy might even set in or their standards may drop because of fear if they are not strong enough.

God shows us that He is a caring and a loving God. He caters to the sick, the lost, the lonely, the helpless, and the dying. Even when they nailed him to the cross, He was able to look with compassion at these very same people who mocked Him, spit on Him, beat Him, called Him all sorts of names, and in the end crucify Him, and He said to His Heavenly Father forgive them for they know not what they have done.

Look at Ruth in the Bible. Ruth denounced her pagan gods and then accepted Naomi and her God. She adamantly told Naomi, her mother-in-law, that she was not going to leave her and wherever she laid her head that was where she would be also. Boaz, who was very affluent, stood afar, observing and admiring how Ruth was selflessly attending to her mother-in-law. He liked what he saw and made provision for her, unknown to her. He later married her, and this started the bloodline for Jesus.

We read that Uriah, the Hittite (Beersheba's husband), showed loyalty to his fellow workers and his commander-in-chief. When he was summoned to come home by King David to be with his wife, he slept outside under the open sky in solidarity with his fellow people who were also sleeping outside under the open sky miles and miles away. This dedication cost him his life.

Last but not least, we look at our own apostles of New Vision of Hope Ministries. They watched as people talk about them behind their backs, and some walked out on them. God allowed our apostles to pray for people and see them healed or blessed, and they, the apostles, are still waiting for their healing, restoration, and blessings. Even with all of what is going on with their health and what they are facing in their personal lives, they are still able to show love. Everyone who comes by the church speaks about the love they received from both the apostles and the church. They still have a *yes* for God and His work despite what they have gone through and are still going through. They have not wavered in their love and faith for God.

All these examples demonstrate various kinds of character. When you go through trials and tribulation, you are tested, and that will bring out your true character. This character will manifest itself and will show just how strong you are and how much you can endure. This tells a story about the individual—how deeply rooted he or she is in God. Your word(s) are very important, and what you say you should mean. You will act a certain way, and it will be seen and felt. Your word should stand. It says who you are, and it speaks volumes. There is a saying that action speaks louder than words. There is another saying also that your character will take you places where your education cannot.

Now, the same should apply to the covenant relationship we have with God. God has kept His word to us, and what He is asking is that we keep our word to Him. We are to give back 10 percent of our time, money, and talent and a freewill offering back to Him, to his house, the church. This is to enable the church's overhead expenses to be met. Our ministers are to be looked after. Most important, souls can come into His house and be saved, delivered, and set free. He promised us that if we keep His promise and our covenant to Him, He would open the heavens and pour out a blessing so large we will not have room enough to hold it. (Mal. 3:10).

Give to God what belongs to him. Everything in this world is His anyway. We are just caretakers of what He has allowed us to have. All He is saying to us is to give back 10 percent, and the other 90 percent is ours.

CHAPTER 2
The Supernatural and the Anointing

§

THE BIBLE
Bible (N)

- The collection of sacred writings of the Christian religion, comprising the Old and New Testaments.

AGAIN, GOD IS DEALING WITH the total person—that total person is the spiritual and the natural. I like what Joel Osteen who is the Senior Pastor of Lakewood church in Houston, Texas, would say before he starts his sermon. His signature style is that he would tell a joke, and then he would say, "This is my Bible—I am what it says I am, I have what it says I have, and I can do what it says I can do."

With the natural person, we feed our bodies three main meals per day with snacks in between. How many times per day do we feed our spiritual person by reading the Bible? Why can't we do the same with our spiritual life? You might ask how we feed our spiritual life. We do this by reading the Word, fasting, and praying. We also should praise our God. When the praises go up, the blessings come down. As it is in the natural, so should it be in the spiritual. Just like how we dedicate part of our lives to mortal obligations, so we should with our spiritual life. After all, God is the owner and provider of everything in this world. God is the one who will be there when others turn their backs on us. It is also our ticket to get into heaven and to live a victorious life here on earth.

This book, the Bible, is living water to the believer. It is a university all by itself. It deals with history. It tells about creation, life, how to live—and live in such a way that you will be victorious once you have your mind focused on God. It also informs us what will happen if we do not focus on God or accept Him as our Lord and Savior.

This book, the Word, the Bible, gives clear instructions on right and wrong. It tells the past and the present and foretells the future, what is going to happen, things to come. It also gives us instructions on how to present our gifts in the form of tithes and offerings and the different types of offerings so that they are presentable and acceptable to God our Father, who is the Creator of the world and everything that is in the world.

The Bible is hope to the hopeless, healing to the sick, comfort to the disheartened, and life to the dying. It is all that and more to those who believe. To the ungodly (sinners), it is just another book to question.

The Bible suggests faith—believing in the sovereign God by its people. Some of the things it speaks about are

- **Tithes** Malachi 3:3–4;
- **Prosperity** Genesis 12:15–16;
- **Poverty** Exodus 22:25–27;
- **Money** 1 Timothy 6:10;
- **Provision To The Poor** Psalm 140:12;
- **Increases** Colossians 1:10;
- **Honesty** Proverbs 19:1;
- **Giving And Receiving** Proverbs 22:9, Psalm 84:11;
- **Stewardship** Luke 12:42–44;
- **Blessings** Genesis 12:2, Deuteronomy 1:11;
- **Curses** Malachi 3:9;
- **Vows** Genesis 28:20–21;
- **Wealth** Genesis 30:43;
- **Sacrifices** Leviticus 3:1; and
- **Death** Proverbs 18:21, just to mention a few.

Are you tithing the same amount of your time to the Word of God by reading your Bible, or are you robbing God of your **time** in His Word? The next question is how many time(s) you feed your spiritual person as opposed to your natural person? When compared, which is more of a priority based on your action, and do you have the same zest and enthusiasm? (A thought to ponder.)

My suggestion to you is that you start to invest your time in God's Word so that the spiritual person can become edified.

WORDS
Words (N)

- A unit of language, consisting of one or more spoken sounds or their written representation that functions as a principal carrier of meaning.
- A speech or talk to express one's emotion in words.

Words are spirit. We can hear it when spoken, but we cannot physically touch it. The Bible states that it is sharper than a two-edge sword. The sword will cut the outward physical body, and that wound, if looked after early, can heal. The body also has a natural component built into it to heal superficial wounds. However, words will go past the outer physical body and enter the inner spiritual area, the mind. This area cannot be seen by the naked eyes.

I remember two little boys when I was in the school system in Jamaica as a counsellor. They were always dirty looking. Their clothes were dirty, and they walked around looking dejected; they had no friends. They would skip school, ride the buses, and hang out in the park downtown all day. They were failing. Notice I did not say they were failures.

I got a hold of the two little boys and started to counsel them, telling them how God considers them beautiful and they were wonderfully made. There is greatness in them, and it is important to believe in themselves. I told them they were no mistake, and God loved them.

I started seeing changes in them just like you would when a caterpillar changes into a butterfly. Caterpillars bump, push, wiggle, and slide forward to the cracked area of the shell that lets in the light. They start eating this shell. This shell cannot hold back the change that is taking place—the change from a caterpillar to that beautiful butterfly that wants to come out and eventually will come out and be free.

Those two boys started to come back to school. Their clothes were now clean. They started to participate in class. They were bubbling with enthusiasm, excitement, and assurance on the inside. When the teacher asked the class questions, they would put their hands up, but before the teacher could ask them or anyone else, they would shout out the answer for the question asked. You know what? The answers they gave were right. It was to the point where their teachers came and asked me if I could counsel them to tone them down so they would give the other children a chance to answer. The power of positive spoken words.

What I am trying to say is words have a lot of power. Be careful what you allow and who you allow to speak into your life or over your life. I was a new babe in the Lord and did not understand a lot, especially about the spiritual aspect of life. However, I was a follower of my inner voice. I later learned this is the Holy Spirit.

The Bible says in Proverbs 18:21 that there is life and death under the tongue. If you speak positively, life comes forth. If you speak negatively, death will come. Death does not just mean closing your eyes and being buried six feet under the earth to rot. Death can mean you no longer go forth with power. You become crippled in your thoughts and movements. You become stagnant, almost useless.

God says in Exodus 3:14, "Believe that I am who I say I am, and believe who I say you are. You are heir to His throne, you are a child of God." God says you are great from within because you have Him on the inside. You have His Word.

God also says that words without action are dead. You must have faith, and even if it is as small as a mustard seed, it is OK. It is enough.

We see this demonstrated where David's stone was small and smooth, but it killed the giant Goliath, and David was able to cut off his head. No longer will that giant hold you down with fear.

God says, "You do your part and I will do my part." That is a promise. God's Word says to have faith and trust Him. Luke 6:38 says, "Give and it shall be given back to you, good measure, pressed down, shaken together and running over." **Give what?** Give 10 percent of your time, 10 percent of you talent, and 10 percent of your gross income and a freewill offering, where the freewill offering is an amount of your choice, to the church. This is to enable His work to continue, pastors and the needy are taken care of, and His house can be maintained. Souls can come into His Kingdom, and they can be saved, set free, and delivered.

You do all this, and God says in Hebrews 13:5 that He will never leave you nor forsake you. He also says He will pour out a blessing so large that you will not have room enough to store it. A blessing here can be financial, healing, deliverance, and/or favor irrespective of what is happening around you and the world at large.

Former President Obama said in one of his speeches to some college graduates, "When in doubt, speak about it." Again, the power of words. If you can see it, believe it, and then you will achieve it. That is why it is important that you read God's Word daily. It will be the difference between life and death, which is based on your action and reaction. It will manifest itself in your life. Words are positively therapeutic.

SPIRIT
Spirit (N)

- The principle of conscious life; the vital principle in humans, animating the body or mediating between body and soul
- The soul regarded as separating from the body at death
- The third person of the Trinity; Holy Spirit
- Often, spirits. A strong distilled alcoholic liquor

We are spiritual beings housed in a human body having a natural experience. Almost everything about us is spiritual. When we speak, words are uttered from our mouth. We can hear the words but we cannot physically feel or touch them. Likewise with sounds. We hear them, but we cannot physically touch them. The brain is another area. It is a big mass with a lot of activities taking place. Some we can explain, and others we cannot explain. There is coding, decoding, processing, interpreting, submitting, and producing going on. All is created by the source, and all is connected to the source. The source is God the Father, God the Son, and God the Holy Spirit. In the Bible, it says God is a Spirit, and they that worship Him must worship Him in Spirit and truth. So the Christian walk is a spiritual walk. 2 Corinthians 5:7 states, "We walk by faith, and not by sight." This leads us to faith, and faith is a spirit. Faith is a confidence or trust in a person or thing. We cannot touch it. It is something we know that we know on the inside.

God is a Spirit, and He prepares for us spiritually. As Christians, we have a spiritual connection to God. He knew us before we were born—before He created us. He made us great, and we have greatness on the inside; He created great things for us. He said that He would not withhold something good from us. We have to believe and walk into this greatness. He said even if our faith is as small as a mustard seed, that by faith, we can speak to our mountain and say be thou removed, and by faith, it will. He also said to call that which is not as though it is. For example, let the weak say I am strong, and let the poor say I am rich. He also said if we can see it and believe it, then it will be as we have said.

That is why we as Christians have to believe that God is who He says He is. It is important that we believe what God's Word says, and we should do what His Word tells us to do. There is a blessing in our obedience to His Word. He said if we give, it would be given back to us, pressed down and running over. One type of giving is your tithes and offerings. He said to give 10 percent of your time, 10 percent of your talent, and 10 percent of your income as tithes to His house, the church, so that others like yourself will come into His Kingdom, be saved, be delivered, and be set free. The pastors, widows, and orphans can be taken care of. He also asked that we give a freewill offering for the upkeep and maintenance of the ministry.

God says if we give, He will open the windows of heaven and pour out such a blessing that we will not have room enough to receive it. A blessing here can be financial, healing, and/or favor. One move from God can drop an idea or favor that can cause life changes. For example, from the pit to the palace, from a nobody to a somebody. From a life-threatening disease to perfectly good health. Doors opening that would otherwise have been closed. God is limited only by the limitation of your faith.

There is a saying that words without action are dead. Your giving and the amount you give will demonstrate how spiritually connected you are to your source, who is God Almighty. He paid the ultimate price: He died on the cross and shed His Blood for us so that our sins could be washed away, which by the way, He did not commit, and we are redeemed back to Him.

A mother whose son had once believed in God and dressed properly had started to believe less and less in God after going to college. He was not well groomed anymore, and he wore sandals as shoes. He returned home from college and asked his mother if she could see God. She said no. He asked if she could touch God like how he can touch her. She said no. He told her he would start dressing properly if she could prove God is there. His mother prayed that night and asked God for help and guidance.

In the middle of the night, she heard her son cry out. As a mother, she naturally ran to his room. He told her he had a toothache, and the pain was moving up and down his face. At that moment, God dropped an idea in her spirit.

She asked her son if he could see the pain, and he said no. Can you touch the pain? He said no. She said how do you know that the pain is there? He said he knew because the pain was moving up and down his face.

Her response to him was, son, the same way you know the pain is there because you can feel the pain is the same way I know that God is there because I can feel Him moving. Needless to say, her son became a born-again believer that night. You just know that God is there, and you can sense His presence. It is a spiritual connection.

THE BLOOD
Blood (N)

- The fluid that circulates in the principal vascular system of humans beings and other vertebrates, in humans consisting of plasma in which the red blood cells, white blood cells, and platelets are suspended.

Come with me and let me carry you on this journey.

There must be a creator, a mastermind before and behind the world. The Bible says God spoke this world into existence, and for humans, He blew his own breath into us and His Blood flows inside of us.

When we sinned, God allowed his son, who was sinless, to die on the cross for our sins. That Blood, which was shed for you and I, has allowed a Blood-covenant relationship to form and take place between God and humankind.

Procreation first starts with a sperm and an egg fusing together and becoming one. It travels up and attaches itself to the womb of the female where it is connected to the blood. This blood nourishes the fetus in the womb to maturity. It carries food and oxygen to the cells and takes away all waste and impurities from the cells. As the songwriter says "That Blood that gives you strength from day to day—it will never lose its Power." The birth of humankind is established and fulfilled. We have the birth of God's creation: *man*—man here meaning male and female—being born.

Sacrifices

After birth, all it takes is for humankind to have faith, openly accept Christ, who is the Source, and become covered under His Blood. We now have a covenant relationship with God, and we are covered by His Blood—*the Blood* that gives you strength from day to day, and it will never, never lose its *power*.

All you have to do is have faith, and the Bible says if your faith is as small as a mustard seed, by faith you can say to your mountain to be thou removed and it will. Here, a mountain is any difficulty, sickness, problem(s), or diseases you have to face. A mustard seed, on the other hand, is the smallest seed, but when planted, it grows to be the largest and tallest tree in the forest. If you look up the properties of a mustard seed, it can cure quite a number of sicknesses and diseases; therefore, if your faith is as small as a mustard seed, you can speak to your mountain by faith to be thus removed, and it will be. Whether it is a spoken word that gives encouragement, an idea dropped into your spirit that when applied will take you out of your present situation, or you are healed supernaturally of your diseases or sicknesses. God can give you extraordinary favor from people and places you never imagined. You will also get that strength and peace of mind to know that you will be able to go through and face your crisis. All this is because you have a covenant relationship with God. All He asks is that you accept Him as your personal Savior, have faith, and give back to Him 10 percent of your time, money, and talent as tithes and offerings. This 10 percent is holy.

Christ is the bridge between the biblical time back then and present time now. He is the sacrificial lamb that was crucified for you and me. No longer do we have to sacrifice animals to speak to God as in biblical times. We can boldly go to the throne, give our petition to God, and know that He hears us and will answer our prayer(s). We do not have to go to a priest and have him go to God on our behalf anymore. We can go straight to God ourselves. All He asks is that we be good stewards and give 10 percent of all we receive to continue his work of getting souls into His Kingdom, and the other 90 percent is ours. He is not a man; He cannot lie. Numbers 23:19 says, "God is not a man that he should lie; neither the Son of man that he should repent: hath he said it, and shall he not do it? Or hath he spoken, and shall he not do it?" So trust Him and see if He will not open the windows of heaven and pour out a blessing that you will not have room enough to receive. Trust Him and see His glory manifest in your life, pressed down, shaken together, and running over.

Have faith in Him and take Him as your Lord and Savior, and see if He will not lead you into a victorious life. Present your gift(s) and offerings in a presentable manner as stated by God.

Believe that you are covered by the Blood. You are who God says you are; you can do what He says you can do, and you have what He says you have.

Be the best you can, to all the people you can, in every way you can. Trust and have faith in God and watch Him move on your behalf.

CHAPTER 3
Blockage to the Flow of God

〰

Habit
Habit (N)

- An acquired behavior pattern regularly followed until it has become almost involuntary
- Customary practice or use
- A particular practice, custom, or usage

A HABIT IS FORMED AFTER repetitive action over time. Once the action becomes embedded in us, then it forms a part of our character. Based on that, we will act a certain way. This behavior can be determined or identified to be good or bad, negative or positive.

Because we are dealing with tithes and offerings, I am going to focus on that area. God requires us under the covenant agreement to pay 10 percent of everything we have acquired to Him. That is, our money, talent, time, and a freewill and cheerful offering. God's intention is for the church to meet its overhead expenses, maintain the church, and take care of the pastors. The money, time, and talent are intended to also meet the needs of the people who will come into the church, especially the orphans, widows, poor, and lost.

The negative side of all this is that some people do not want to give or pay their 10 percent, so they make up the excuse that pastors are using the money for their personal uses. That is, they use the money to buy big cars and houses and live a big lifestyle. Although this might be true for some pastors who come in with the wrong motive(s), this is not true for all churches and pastors.

The fact of the matter is that we should not watch what others are doing or saying. We, however, should focus on having a personal relationship with God and follow His instructions, and our desire should be to win souls for His Kingdom. We also want to do what is right in the sight of God. We do this by doing our part and letting God do the judging. After all, each person will have to answer to God about his or her own actions. God will do the judging and administer the punishment.

When you do your part by contributing your time, talent, and money, you are giving to God, keeping the relationship alive and the covenant between you and God. He said you should give with a cheerful and willing heart, and then you will see if He will not pour out a blessing you will not have room enough to receive. Blessing here represents money, good health, long life, prosperity, favor with people, and favor with God. The decisions you make now will not only affect you but your next generation up to the fourth generation.

If you are guilty, you can start changing your attitude and your mind-set. You start changing by identifying what is holding you back and making a conscious decision to change. At first it will appear difficult, but if you press and stick to your decision, you can overcome. You have to press past the pain because at first, it will seem difficult to keep up, but as you press and remain focused, it will get easier, and you will eventually change the bad habit and the new habit will become a reality. If you continue to do something repeatedly, it will eventually develop into a habit. Positive habits bring about positive returns and rewards. A new character will form, thus creating a new you. A new and positive person will emerge also.

If you make an effort to continuously pay your tithes and offerings each week, whether on a fortnight or monthly basis depending on how you get your money or your pay, then it will become easy and not seem like a chore anymore. Over time, you will find it a pleasure to give. We in our church have experienced what a pleasure it is to give. We also experienced and have seen the response from those we have the pleasure of blessing. The experience was priceless and awesome. So, do what is right in God's sight. Give your time, talent, and money to God's house, share with God's people, and see how He will bless you.

Addiction
Addict

- (N) A person who is addicted to an activity, habit, or substance
- (V) To habituate or abandon (oneself) to something compulsively or obsessively

You might ask how relevant this is to tithes and offerings. The fact is when you should be giving to God and his work, your attention is caught up with your addiction or agenda, and God's work is neglected.

Let me highlight some of the areas that a person is or can become addicted: drugs, pornography, drinking, smoking, gambling, anger, shopping, food, sex, and gossip just to name a few. You become totally engulfed and consumed with this addiction.

No matter what it is, it has the person under control. It is like a tight hold, and it is very hard to break that habit. You want to stop but are unable to. You try to stop but go right back. It has a strong hold on your life. You know it, that it is wrong, and you feel it, but you cannot resist it. It causes pain, anxiety, and loss in your life because you are not doing the right things you should be doing. It causes you to rob God of your tithes and offerings, talent, and your time. You are cheating your family, and most times, you end up losing them. The improvements and achievements you should gain in your life are on hold because you are not where you should be mentally and physically.

I was there with shopping, so I can emphatically tell you that not all is lost. Start to refocus on God and ask for His help and forgiveness. Ask Him for His guidance. He can change things, and what was meant for evil, He can turn it around for good. 1 Peter 5:7 states, "Cast all your care upon him; for he careth for you."

Put God first and He will direct your path. Sometimes you even have to drop some people out of your life. The places you used to go, you can no longer go, and the things you use to do, you stop doing them. Know that the same powerful force that was in Christ is in you. It will make you victorious.

I was there with my shopping, and God showed me how to start getting out of debt. You know what—it worked. I am not 100 percent there yet, but I am a work in progress, and I am certainly not where I was. Where I could not pay my tithes and offerings before, I am able to do so now. I am able to see the light at the end of the tunnel, where before it was total darkness. God has turned it around, and now He is using me. I am able to tell someone with **assurance** that God has taken me out, and He certainly can do the same for you.

Focus on God; He has a whole lot waiting for you. Get your mind off your problem(s) and get involved with the things of God. He will turn it around for your good. Numbers 23 states, "He is not a man that He should lie; hath He not said it, will He not do it?" Renew your covenant relationship with God because you are the one who wandered off and got sidetracked. He was always there waiting for you with outstretched arms to come back to Him.

I know it is hard, and you might have a relapse here or there. When that happens, just pick up the pieces, however hard it might seem, and put one foot forward a day at a time. God will send you help.

God is saying, "Put Me first! Trust Me and my promise to you! Test Me! Prove Me." God is saying, "I will be faithful to open the windows of blessing of my abundance to you! I am bound to you by my Word! You will receive all that I have promised when you remain faithful and obedient to Me" (Mal 3:8–10).

So do what is right, start paying your tithes and offerings, and make God and the things of God your focus and priority.

STRUGGLES
Struggle (V)

- To contend with an adversary or opposing force
- To contend resolutely with a task, problem
- To advance with violent effort
- To be coping with inability to perform well or to win; contend with difficult

In the beginning, God created the earth and put Adam as a man and Eve as a woman to inhabit the Garden of Eden where everything was provided for them. After they sinned, they were put out of the garden so they would not find the tree that is called the **Tree of Life**. God told them that by the sweat of their brow, man shall eat bread and the woman shall have pain during childbirth. This lets us know that there will be some form of struggling in life. However, when God shed His Blood for us, He redeemed us back to Him and the throne, and we are now living under Grace.

Struggles are a battle of the mind. A lot of our struggles are created by us when we yield to the flesh. The flesh is very selfish and full of pride. The flesh will tell us we need something right away and we have to have it now. The flesh deals with the here and now, instant gratification. The flesh does not think about tomorrow; it is not practical. This indecisive manner is what causes the struggle. We are uncertain about what decision(s) to make. It is between right and wrong, now or later, good or evil. A few times, we also put our mountain(s) too high, and then we have to struggle to maintain and stay on top of this mountain.

The point is that there is a time for everything, and God's way and timing are always right and always on time, and they have fewer struggles.

We have to believe and know that no two persons are alike even if they are identical twins. Our DNA and our fingerprints will never be the same. Some chromosome although it appears similar will be different, thus causing us to be different and unique. God looked at His masterpiece, His crowned jewel, His creation of humanity in His image with His breath breathing into us, and He said it was good. He made some people tall, some short, and some fat. He gave gifts to each person, and He gave equally to everyone the same amount of time within the day, which is twenty-four hours. A few use these gifts, becoming very creative in using these gifts to improve themselves and acquire many assets. There are those who cannot accept their physical appearance and opt to change it. Then others just sit on their gifts, become lazy, and do nothing.

Regardless of whom we are or become, we have some form of struggles. This can cause us to overextend ourselves, at times to the point where we cannot meet our obligations to God, His work, His church, His Kingdom, and even our families.

Our gracious, loving, and forgiving God says when we find ourselves in this predicament and struggle to call on Him and He will answer. Ephesians 2:10 states, "For we are His workmanship, created in Christ Jesus unto good works, which God hath before ordained that we should walk in them." He walks beside you through your darkest challenges and troubles you struggle with. He said His burden is lighter and easier. He will never leave us or forsake us. He will direct our path. We are to seek Him and He will be found. In Matthew 6:33, He also said to seek Him first and His Kingdom and His righteousness and everything will be added to us, pressed down, and running over. We will not have room enough to receive it.

How do we do this? First, confess our sins to God and have faith that He is who He says He is. He created us and bought us with a price. His Blood was shed for us so He could redeem us back to Him. Love your neighbor and His church as you love yourself and as Christ loves the church. Give 10 percent of your time, 10 percent of your talent, and 10 percent of your gross income and a freewill offering so people who

Sacrifices

are at a loss can find their way back into the Kingdom of God. They can be set free and delivered like you and I were, and His work and the ministry will be able to continue.

God loves us equally. He said no one is more important than the other is. We see this demonstrated in our own bodies. In our body, no member is more important. The area that is considered the least, for example, is our buttock; if this area was closed down, our entire body would close down, and we would die. So God made that area dignified, and people have to give respect to that area and treat it well. So if you have struggles, give them to God and become free. What was meant for evil, God will turn it around for your good.

The more we lean to our own understanding and ways, the more our struggles will be—the more we will get ourselves in debts, crisis, sickness, and situations. Lean on God instead. Today, rest in the knowledge that God is with you. Whatever the circumstances you may face, you have nothing to fear.

WEAKNESS/WEARINESS
Weakness (N)

- A self-indulgent liking or special fondness, as for a particular thing
- An object of special desire; something very difficult to resist

Weary (A)

- Physically or mentally exhausted by hard work, exertion, strain, etc., fatigued, tired
- Impatient or dissatisfied with something or impatient

Everyone can identify a time in his or her life when he or she felt weak and vulnerable or where he or she had over extended his- or herself.

You might have set goals but have not been able to attain those goals due to not enough funds, a loss from your job, or a loss of a love one. This can cause you not to be able to meet your demands or pay your bills and pay them on time. Not to mention your tithes and offerings. Whatever the reason, there is weariness, lack of appetite, lack of enthusiasm, and neglect in meeting obligations. This is not good because all our money and everything we own belong to God. Of the 100 percent of what He has allowed us to acquire, all God is asking for is 10 percent. Ten percent of your time, talent, and money. The other 90 percent is yours.

We look at Esther in the Bible in the book of Esther. She felt lonely, afraid, and weak. She expressed this when she was forced to go to the king and talk to him about her people, who were destined to die by the hand of Haman, who hated the Jews. Even though she was not summoned by the king, in those days, if the king did not summon you and he turned down that golden cup when you appeared, you could be killed.

Some things you have to do through prayer and fasting, and this she did. God has placed within our hands the powerful weapons of fasting and prayer. They are capable of moving God's hand. She prayed and fasted for three days and sent the word that all Jews should do the same. First, she believed there is a God. She did not focus on her lack because whatever you focus on inside will manifest itself on the outside and determine our actions. She called upon God. Matthew 7:7 says, "Ask and it shall be given, seek and he shall find, knock and it shall be open."

Your Creator wants good things to happen to you. James 1:17 says, "Every good gift and every perfect gift is from above, and cometh down from the Father of lights, with whom is no variableness, neither shadow of turning."

Call on God, surrender, and ask Him for direction. He will start to show you how to get out of debt. He will direct you how to be good stewards of your money—or should I say His money. He will let you become the victor instead of the victim in your situation. In Esther's situation, her people, the Jews, were saved from being killed, and Haman and his family were killed instead.

This shows that when we admit our weakness to God, we activate His compassion. Independence from our Creator, the power above, will always birth a tragedy. When God starts to get you out of debt, you have to remember the things of God. Remember your tithes and offerings. Offer your talent and your time also. In the Bible, God says that when you take care of the things of God, He will withhold nothing good from you. In fact, He will open the windows of heaven and pour out a blessing that we will not have room enough to receive (Mal. 3:10).

We live in a busy, hurried world, and it is easy to get caught up in the whirlwind of busyness, tasks, and goals. The atmosphere you permit will determine the product you will produce. Many people know they are lacking something but few discover what it is. Put God first; make Him a priority in your life and watch God work on your behalf. God's challenge is to *prove Him* (Mal. 3:8–11).

One method that God uses today to pour upon His people is the return from the tithes. Is it any wonder that this is the one area that Satan has hindered the majority of Christians from receiving God's promised blessing? If the enemy can cause you to withhold giving your tithes and offerings, then he will succeed in binding your finances.

In God's plan for supernatural provision, He intends the *tithes* to be the means whereby He blesses and bestows prosperity on His people and from which the needs of His house will be supplied. The tithes are also a vital part of your relationship with him. Through the system of giving tithes, there should be *no lack in the house of God and no lack with his people.*

OBSTRUCTION
Obstruction (N)

- The deliberate delaying or preventing a process or change

If we have not been paying our tithes and offerings as we should, guilt can cause us to become depressed, even to the point of dropping out. In this life, the Bible states that the devil came only to steal, kill, and destroy like a thief in the night. We find that most times he uses the people who are close to us, such as our family, friends, and even our church family, to knock us farther down when we fall. The reason being that these people we let into our personal space know our secrets. Our enemy, on the other hand, we will not allow to get close to us or even near our personal space.

Our mind is another area that can become an obstruction when we have sinned and especially when we have done something that we consider wrong.

We may have asked God for forgiveness, which from the moment we ask Him, He has forgiven us, but we cannot forgive ourselves. We beat ourselves down instead of picking up the pieces, moving forward, and starting or are willing to make changes. According to Matthew 15:11, "Not that which goeth into the mouth defileth a man, but that which cometh out of the mouth, this defileth a man." God looks at the heart because whatever you think, all that you do, and all that you say comes from the heart.

The Bible says that you must give 10 percent of you tithes, talent, and time to the Lord. If you fall short, just confess to God and ask for His forgiveness, His directions, and guidance to help you to be able to do and get all these things right the next time around. Get back on track, and your fears and unbelief will be gone. Start doing what is right. If you ask Him for directions, He will help you and direct your path. He is limited only by your failure to look to Him and expect His supernatural provision(s) in your life. All resources of heaven are at Jesus's disposal. He had not worldly wealth, yet He possessed an abundance of *all* that He needed from his Father's supernatural provision. God will take whatever you have whenever you offer it to Him, and He will multiply it to meet your needs and His. He cares for you.

So do what is right and pay your tithes and offerings to the Lord.

Psalm 35:27 states, "Let them show for joy, and be glad, that favour my righteous cause: yea, let them say continually, Let the Lord be magnified, which hath pleasure in the prosperity of His servants."

Hindrance
Hindrance (N)

- Obstruction or hold back
- An impeding, stopping, preventing, or the like
- The state of being hindered
- A person or thing that hinders

When God created us, He created us in such a way that we are able to think (be creative) and do things (accomplish) that which comes as an idea, a dream, or an imagination into the mind. We are able to do all this because He breathed His breath into us. Our God is a big, awesome, and powerful God. He is because He was the one who created the world and brought us into existence. Therefore, we can be all He says we can be and do all He says we can do.

After all the teachings we have received, some people still allow the devil, people, and their fears to get into their spirit and become a hindrance to them.

One way we can beat this hindrance in our spirit from taking over is to believe in God's strength and His Word. Wait on Him even when we find ourselves getting tired and weary. We have to trust God. Joseph went from the pit to prison to the palace. He never lost his faith. We are sometimes a stubborn and hardheaded people. We have to learn, however, to trust God. While we are waiting on God, we were told that we should get busy and become involved with the things of God and stay firm in that situation and struggle. God will give us power, and He will increase our ability and our strength. He is a big God and our covenant God.

When we see our weaknesses, we should not allow ourselves to begin to lose hope and give up. Instead, we need to look at it as an opportunity for God to show up and give us power.

2 Corinthians 12:9 says, "And he said unto me, my grace is sufficient for thee: for my strength is made perfect in weakness. Most gladly therefore will I rather glory in my infirmities, that the power of Christ may rest upon me." God is saying that in my weakness, He gives power.

Isaiah 40:31 says, "But they that wait upon the Lord shall renew their strength; they shall mount up with wings as eagle; they shall run, and not be weary: and they shall walk, and not faint." Have an expectation that God will move on your behalf.

We see an example of this with Ruth and Boaz. She waited patiently, and while waiting, she got busy in helping her mother-in-law and remained faithful. We saw how God blessed her in the end when she got Boaz as her husband. By faith, we have to bind ourselves together with and in Christ and be one with Him.

Wait on God and expect Him to do something on your behalf. Have an expectation, not like Abraham and Sarah, who got tired of waiting on the promise, wanted to push the promise forward in their timing, and do it themselves instead of waiting on God. They stopped expecting the promise to happen and in their mess caused a lot of confusion.

At times, things can get discouraging, and you start losing faith. The messages we hear reaffirm that while we wait, we have to keep believing. Keep having faith and believe that God will do what He said He would do. The faith you have inside should rise up, and you must never give up but keep expecting God to perform. Everything is yours already from inception, when God created us and when He died on the cross and His Blood was shed.

He will give you new strength. He is constantly taking care of you. The waiting process allows you to grow. You are going to wait on the Lord. In His timing, He is working out your situation and the solution that is best for you. One Kings 17:14 says, "For thus said the Lord God of Israel, the barrel of meal shall not waste, neither shall the crude of oil fail, until the day that the Lord sendeth rain upon the earth." What He expects is that you will keep your covenant obedience and pledge to Him while you wait.

Galatians 5:7 states, "Ye did run well; who did hinder you that ye should not obey the truth?"

Therefore, show your strength by doing what is right by paying your tithes and offerings and have expectation of God's promises.

Limits
Limits (N)

- Boundary
- Something that restrains or confines

When we consider how this world came into existence, we can't help but know that there must be a superior mind behind all this creation. There is awesomeness in the grandeur of this world. We cannot imagine the depth of this person's imagination. We read that this person is *God*. He spoke this world into existence, breathed His breath into us, and said everything is good, and it is indeed good. Yet with all this exhibition of creativeness, we still doubt God. We consider at times that we are bigger than God is and that we can handle our problem(s) by ourselves better than God can. We have to learn to start believing God. Believe deeply that God is who He says He is. We have seen miracles, and miracles happen around us, to others, and even to ourselves. Yet we find it hard to believe.

I am standing before you as one of God's miracle babies. What He says He will do, He will do. He has worked in my life and is still working in my life. I am a work in progress. The last set of miracles God did in my life—but certainly not the last set of miracles God will do for me—was to take me out of debt. You heard me confess how much in debt I was in. Although I was paying my bills on time, I was finding it hard to pay my tithes and offerings. It started to become an obstacle and a battle to fight. When I sought God's help and openly admitted to robbing Him and asked Him for His forgiveness, He not only forgave me but also showed me how to get out of debt. He turned it around and now uses me to teach about the same very thing I was guilty of not doing, which is not paying my tithes and offerings. Something that was meant to destroy me is now being used to elevate me. Because I have decided to and made a conscious effort to change and for God to use me, He has even gone further. He made provisions and blessed me with one of the desires of my heart: a new Lexus NX200t from the dealer with a big red bow when I got it. I considered this vehicle with the big red bow a gift from God to me for my Christmas present. He even customized it for me. I had surgery done to my spine a little while back, and this car came with a lumbar adjustable support in the front seats, and these can be customized and adjusted to the comfort and support of my back.

Don't tell me God is not alive and real. You too have to start letting go and letting God. You have to know that you know that God can do the impossible, and He will make a way when it seems that there is no way. He makes the impossible possible. You have to take the limits off God and start to trust and believe Him and His Word.

His plan for us is to live a long, healthy, and victorious life in all areas. He made provisions for everyone before we were born. Adam and Eve were put in the garden with everything they could ever desire at their disposal. When they sinned, however, the situation changed, and they were put out of the Garden of Eden. Even though things changed, God still made a way for them and us by allowing His Son Jesus to die on the cross so He could redeem us back to Grace.

All He is asking is that we trust Him, keep His commandments, and keep the covenant relationship we have with Him by accepting Him as our Lord and Savior and giving 10 percent of our time, talent, and tithes and a willing and joyful offering to the ministry. The other 90 percent is ours.

I am facing my financial circumstances today from a position of knowing. I declare that I will be led, directed, and controlled by God's Holy Spirit. As God reveals them to me by His Spirit, I will take hold of them by faith.

Galatians 4:14 says, "And my temptation which was in the flesh ye despised not, nor rejected; but received me as an angel of God, even as Christ Jesus."

Remember, God is bigger than our problem(s). Learn to trust God, let go, take the limits off God, and see if miracles will not start to happen in your life too. Time is everything, and time is the accumulation and duration of our experiences. God will do the miraculous according to His timing when He thinks that we are ready for the miracles in our lives. He will do for you the same way He did for me. Whatever area you are having a problem with, give it to God, and believe and trust Him.

Remember also to pay your tithes and offerings. God is expecting you to do the right thing.

CHAPTER 4
Manifestation and Power of the Living God

§

CHANGES

- Changes (V) are inevitable (incapable of being avoided or escaped).
- To transform or convert
- To substitute another or others for, exchange for something else, usually of the same kind.

CHANGES CAN BE DIFFICULT. SOMETIMES we get comfortable where we are and do not want to change, so we try to resist the change that has come into our lives. We are afraid to leave what we are familiar with. We fear the unknown. However, from the moment we were conceived, changes started taking place. Change is going to happen whether we like it or not. Change is always a temporary position or a minor adjustment that will make a major difference or improvement when we surrender or adapt. From inception inside the womb, there are changes taking place until the womb can no longer hold the fetus, and then we are born. Outside of the womb, the body continues to change, i.e., from a toddler, to a teenager, and on to an adult. At every stage, our body changes and likewise our minds—how we think, what we believe, how we act. As it is in the natural, so it is in the spiritual.

Sacrifices

As we accept Christ as our personal Savior, our spiritual lives start to go through the metamorphosis of changes too. As we read our Bible, pray to God, mediate on His words, and go to church, changes start taking place in our spiritual life and walk. Our faith level begins to rise. We start shedding off the old person and start putting on or embracing the new person. Here we start learning to let go and let God. Here we start learning about God, who He is to us, and what He expects from us. We learn how we are to live, right from wrong. How we are to present our bodies as living sacrifices, holy and acceptable to God. We learn how to present our gifts to Christ (money, talent, time, tithes, and offerings). We learn by faith what to expect from God our Father in heaven in return. We learn to have an expectation.

Malachi 3:8–12 states, "Will a man rob God? Yet ye have robbed me. But ye say. Where have we robbed thee? In tithes and offerings. Ye are cursed with a curse: for ye have robbed me, even this whole nation. Bring ye all the tithes into the storehouse, that there may be meat in mine house, and prove me now herewith, said the Lord of hosts, if I will not open you the windows of heaven, and pour you out a blessing, that there shall not be room enough to receive it. And I will rebuke the devourer for your sakes, and he shall not destroy the fruits of your ground; neither shall your vine cast her fruit before the time in the field, said the Lord of hosts. And all nations shall call you blessed: for ye shall be a delightsome land, said the Lord of hosts."

Evaluate yourselves, and if you have not been doing the right thing, if you have been robbing God, just ***stop*** where you are and start doing the right thing. Ask for His forgiveness and continue moving forward. Do not linger in lo-debar in a sea of unforgiveness to yourself because God has already forgiven you. Lo-debar signifies a place of no productivity, barrenness and isolation. John 15 says, "God will prune us for new growth so we can be more productive and bear more fruit." God likes freshness. He has something great for our future.

Sometimes we have setbacks in life, such as the loss of someone, a job, our home, or a career or we just plain and simple are robbing

God. A season can be over in our lives. Whatever it is, just pick up the pieces, however hard it might seem at first, and just keep moving forward.

Accept the changes in our lives—keep the faith, and God will elevate you. You will learn new sets of skills. He will promote you to higher heights. God knows where you are. He knows how to move you and promote you. He will put people in places for you to give you favor. You have to learn to **let go and let God** and move forward, not stay stagnant where you are. You also have to let go of people who are holding you back. If you do not get rid of the wrong people you have in your life, you won't be able to or have room to meet the right people who are to come into your life.

Change is a must in life. You can deal with it either positively or negatively. The choice is yours. Remember, with God all things are possible. Stay in sync with the plans God has for your life. Stay open. What is meant for evil, He will turn it around for our good. Two Corinthians 3:17 says, "Now the Lord is that Spirit: and where the Spirit of the Lord is, there is liberty."

Remember to pay your tithes and offerings so that another person's life can be changed too.

VALUES
Value (N)

- Relative worth, merit, or importance:
- Monetary or material worth, as in commerce or trade
- The worth of something in terms of the amount of other things for which it can be exchange or in terms of some medium or exchange

God spoke into being the earth and all that is in this world—except humans, which He created from dust and blew his personal breath into.

We are walking around with His DNA. He made us into His image, and He said everything was good.

The first Adam died to sin by succumbing to the devil's temptation and he and his wife Eve eating the forbidden fruit—the apple. The second Adam (*Jesus*) died to take us out of sin and put us back in the King's palace, where we were in the first place and where we rightly belong. The King is our father, Christ, and we are rightful heirs to the throne. Romans 8:17 says, "And if children, heirs; heirs of God, and joint-heirs with Christ; if so be that we suffer with him, that we may be also glorified together."

He knew our names and us before we were born. He even knows how many hairs we have on our head. This is how valuable we are to Him. Matthew 10:30–31 says, "But the very hairs of your head are all numbered. Fear ye not therefore, ye are of more value than many sparrows." How important is God to you and how important are souls to you? How valuable is the Kingdom to us?

We are worth so much to God that He sent his son to die on the cross. He received thirty-nine lashes, and each of those thirty-nine lashes took on our diseases, sicknesses, and sin. Sin He did not commit. Diseases and sicknesses that were never a part of His planning for us. When those lashes cut into His flesh and Blood was drawn, that covenant Blood caused diseases and sicknesses to leave us, and through *faith*, we are healed. Sins are washed away, forgiven, and thrown into the sea of forgetfulness, where they are remembered no more. Somewhere in one of those lashes, you have to believe that you are healed, forgiven, and renewed. The Blood is where it will be renewed—somewhere in those lashes, you will be set free. The song says, the Blood that gives me strength from day to day, it will never lose its *power*.

Take time to talk to someone about God. Take time to do something for and in the ministry to carry forth God's work. Do your part by paying your tithes and contribute your offerings so the church's needs can be met and the things of God can be done. Take time to reach out to someone who is hurting or in need, and in doing so, you also help yourself. It makes a difference to care. That's how valuable you are and that's how important you are.

The world is a stage, and everyone has a part to play. Just consider if each person did his or her part. What a difference it would make. How many lives and souls would be saved? When we do not play our part, we stop or slow down the blessing(s).

The Bible says, "Give and it shall be given back to you; good measure, pressed down, and shaken together, and running over." There is joy in giving and to being able to give also. The reaction from the person getting a blessing from you is priceless and valuable. Money cannot compensate, and there is a certain peace and happiness in knowing you were there for that person or a cause.

You belong to God, and everything you own is His, even the world you are living in, but He is not forcing you to do anything. He said *come* and *give* with a willing and joyful heart. We are important to God, our family, and all the people we encounter one way or another. What we do with this importance will make the difference.

If you do not remember anything I have said thus far, remember this:

YOU ARE IMPORTANT; YOU ARE VALUABLE.

QUALITY
Quality (N)

- Peculiar and essential character, nature, or feature
- Excellence or distinction

When we speak and think about quality, we have to look to God who is a clear example of the standard we should try to aim for. God meticulously, articulately, creatively, calculatedly, intricately, and wonderfully created the human race or species. No one, as creative as we are, is able to duplicate

His artisanship. God said it was good, and indeed, it was good. How He connected the different organs, nerves, veins, arteries, the brain, the heart, and skin to work together—and not to mention the blood, which gives you strength from day to day to function. We can't even imagine. This God is our Creator, and we have a covenant relationship with Him. He is God Almighty. No one is greater than He is. No one is more powerful. He considers us very valuable to Him. Yet we fail to want to please Him, and we question His love for us.

Our aim should be to please Him. In life, we will not please everyone we meet. If we can't please everyone, then we should at least try to please God faithfully and consistently. Man (man here means male and female) will disappoint you or fail you, but God will never do that to you. He is a not a man; He cannot lie. He stands ready to pick us up when we fall or when we call on Him. He requires us to meet the needs of His people. Therefore, if you do what is right and pleasing to God and you are pleased and comfortable with yourself, then you cannot go wrong.

Proverbs 10:22 states, "The blessing of the Lord, it maketh rich, and he addeth no sorrow with it."

One of the things God requires of us is to believe Him, have faith in Him, trust Him and trust in His Word. He also requires us to pay our tithes and our offerings to the church He has given us to become members and where we will be spiritually fed. These tithes and offerings will enable others like ourselves to be able to come in and experience God's blessings. These tithes and offerings are to look after the pastors, widows, orphans, and poor among us. They are also to meet the expenses and maintain the church.

He wants nothing more than to bless you. He said He would withhold nothing good from you. He even said He would honor you with your substances. Proverbs 3:9–10 states, "Honor the Lord with thy substance, and with the first fruits of all thine increases: So shall thy barns be filled with plenty, and thy presses shall burst out with new wine."

God's will for you today is to bring you to a place where you will have plenty—more than enough—and an excess of good things to enjoy.

He said He would even give you the desires of your heart. Malachi 3:10 says, "Bring ye all the tithes into the storehouse, that there may be meat in mine house, and prove me now herewith, saith the Lord of hosts, if I will not open you the windows of heaven, and pour you out a blessing, that there shall not be room enough to receive it." Test Him today and see if He will not open the windows of heaven and pour out a blessing that you will not have room enough to receive.

So today, start focusing on God, and do what is right, i.e., giving 10 percent of your time, talent, tithes, and a freewill offering to the church.

God is your source. He is your provider. He will deliver a quality of life you cannot imagine and like no other can. This is important, and it shows how **valuable** you are to God our King and Father. It shows that He always has you on His mind.

Success
Success (N)

- The attainment of wealth, position, honors, or the like
- The favorable or prosperous termination of attempts or endeavors; the accomplishment of one's goal
- A performance or achievement that is marked by success, as by the attainment of honors

Success is considered a collection of people with different backgrounds coming together, forming different relationships, and pursuing different goals. If you can allow yourself to go there, can you imagine a classroom full of small children and no teachers to teach them or guide them? That is a picture of pure chaos. Imagine a car with no engine. My guess is that this car would not be called a car but instead would be placed in another category and given another name. There is nothing wrong with that. That would be considered another person's goal, idea, or creation. Imagine also if there was no God. Do you realize that without God, there would have been no world? No world would mean no you nor I!

God created greatness all around us. As Mike Murdock said in his book *Secrets of the Richest Man Who Ever Lived*, you must look for it. Expect it. Celebrate it. Pursue it and reward it whenever and wherever it is to be found.

He also said that someone close to you needs something you possess. Likewise, someone else possesses something you need to help you achieve your dreams and your goals. Also, each person around you possesses a different "body of knowledge."

It is your personal responsibility to seek and pursue your desires and goals. No one can do it for you. They can only help you achieve this goal. Proverbs 1:5 teaches, "A wise man will hear, and will increase learning, and a man of understanding shall attain unto wise counsels."

My son Clarence is a very successful entrepreneurial businessperson. While observing him one day as he went about his daily task of pursuing his passion, I realized and observed a few important things in life that will cause one to be successful. It is important that you select a career in life that you enjoy doing. You have to be focused, alert, and willing to go that extra mile to accomplish your goals. You have to be willing and patient to listen to others and to share with others. Share your life, money, wealth, and knowledge. Like you, each person that an individual encounters will possess and impart different knowledge, ideas, and skills because no two persons are alike—no two persons are the same. God created us like that; hence, we end up being totally different. Believe it or not, it makes life more interesting.

I noticed too that when you are anointed to do a task, it does not appear to be a burden. Tasks are performed effortlessly and persons are able to multitask with ease. They are able to think and operate outside the box. In other words, they are very creative. When I look at my son, he is very charismatic in his approach and the way in which he deals with and handles the people with whom he meets.

As you attend to your daily tasks, chores, or activities, you will encounter a wide variety of people. Some will be logical, analytical, critical, or even cynical while others will be creative and energizing, but each person is important and vital to your survival. You have to be savvy enough to be able to size up people and know when to release those people from your life, especially those who will cause you to lose focus.

On the other hand, there are those who will be an asset to you. These people will celebrate you and your achievements and will be instrumental in helping you reach your destiny in life. There is a saying that no man is an island; no man stands alone. Each man is a brother, and each man is a friend.

Even though it is important for us to succeed, God requires us to love the people around us. He requires us to give a helping hand, pour into the lives of others, and help them to succeed in life, and as much as you can, help them to reach their destiny in life also. When you pour into others, as you help them to succeed, God will pour into you and will help you achieve your desires and reach you goals.

We see examples of this in Solomon's life, which is mentioned in the Bible. He had the ability and the patience to listen to others, and his decisions depended on that ability and quality. If you can do this, you will become successful just like Solomon, who was the wisest and most successful person on earth. There are none like him and there will never be another on earth as wise and as successful as he was. God said it.

The Bible shows that Solomon invested in God first, and it showed how much he valued God's people and how much he invested in God's people. Solomon said in 1 Kings 3:9–10, "Give, therefore thy servant an understanding heart to judge thy people, that I may discern between good and bad: for who is able to judge this thy so great a people? And the speech please the Lord, that Solomon had asked this thing."

As God prepares you, prepare for God and His people by paying your tithes and offerings. This will allow God's work to continue in the church, meet the needs of His people, and cause changes and success to His people. You will in turn reap the rewards of God's plans He has waiting in store for you. Psalm 35:27 says, "Let the Lord be magnified, which hath pleasure in the prosperity of His servants."

Be wise like Solomon and give to God what belongs to him. Your tithes, which are 10 percent of your time, 10 percent of your talent, and 10 percent of your gross income. Give also a free will offering and do as God instructed you in His Word. Give with love and give with a passion. See if He will not open the windows of heaven and pour out an extraordinary blessing you will not have room enough to receive.

CHAPTER 5
Impossibility Made Possible

LOYALTY
Loyalty (N)

- Faithful adherence to a sovereign (supreme leader), a government, a leader, a cause, etc.
- Connotes sentiment and the feeling of devotion that one holds for one's country, family, friend, creed (any system or doctrine or formula of religious belief, as a denomination)
- Shows support or allegiance—this implies a sense of duty or of devoted attachment or obligation to something or someone

IN THIS SECTION, I WILL speak about loyalty, and I want to concentrate on two people. The first person I want to look at is Jesus. Jesus was on earth in the flesh for thirty-three years. He was allowed to come on earth through humble beginnings by God and mothered by Mary, which enabled Him to have the human experience.

When Martha and Mary lost their brother, Jesus wept with them. In the flesh while Jesus was on earth before He was crucified, Jesus felt the lost and experienced pain just like ordinary folks. He experienced hunger when He went on a forty-day and forty-night fast, so much so that the devil saw it fit to approach Jesus and tempt him. When the time was near for Jesus to be crucified, Jesus looked through His spiritual eyes and saw all the things He was going to face. The Bible states that He sweat drops of blood. On the actual day of His crucifixion, He who had no sin bore the humiliation, the lashes, the pain, the agony, and the suffering for all of us sinners. Not once did Jesus decide He was not going to do it. He was loyal not only to God the Father but to us also. He did this to save us so we could have our rightful place with God in heaven.

The next person I want to focus on is Job. In the book of Job in the Bible, Job was a wealthy and well-respected man in his community. He was a man of good statue, and he supported those whom he met. He was a man of substance. In one day, he lost all his wealth, his health, and all ten of his children. His body was full of sores.

He was so devastated and broken that all he could do was go outside his gates and sit on the ground. In this state and frame of mind, while sitting at his gates, his three friends came to join him. They did not make matters any easier for him because instead of comforting him they just sat, stared at him, and said nothing for three days. When they broke their silence, it was to judge and accuse Job that he must have done something wrong for all this to befall him. Even Job's wife told him to curse God and die. Job listened to none of them; instead, he sought God more and declared his trust in God.

God came through for Job in a mighty and powerful way. God was ready to take revenge on Job's friends. God rebuked and stripped them openly. Job had to step in and beg God to spare them, which He did. Job was restored back to good health. In fact, God gave him double for his trouble. He had more wealth than before, and he was able to father more children. Job was able to give to his friends some of his substance from his newly acquired wealth.

These two stories that I have highlighted show loyalty at the highest level. God knew Job was loyal to Him. Satan approached Him and said that if Job were put to the test, he would curse God. God allowed Satan to test Job. God told Satan that Job would not fail, so he could go ahead and test Job, but he could not touch his soul. Throughout his ordeal, Job proved his loyalty to God. He was ready to die because of the hardship he was facing, but he stood firm on his belief and trust in God.

God on the other hand showed His loyalty to Job and to us, His children. God restored Job to a better and higher position than the former position he had. God will always honor you if you honor Him. God said that if you are not ashamed of Him, He will not be ashamed of you. When you bless him with your substances, your time, your talent, and your tithes and offerings, He promises that He will pour out a blessing you will not have room enough to receive.

God never changes; He will not let us down. He is loyal in and to our relationship with him. For example, God said He could not lie, and to this day, God has not lied.

Deuteronomy 7:9 states, "Know therefore, that the Lord your God is God: He is the faithful God, keeping His covenant of love to a thousand generations of those who love Him and keep his Commandments."

God has not left us on our own; instead, God has given us the Holy Spirit. The Holy Spirit will comfort and guide us in all truth. The Holy Spirit actually lives inside of us.

Hope
Hope (N)

- The feeling that what is wanted can be had or that events will turn out for the best
- Grounds for this feeling in a particular instant
- A person or thing in which expectations are centered
- Something that is hoped for

Hope is a yesterday problem, a futuristic desire with a today's solution, thus allowing something to happen in the present. God is the only one who can fix any problem we have to face. He knows the beginning from the end. He is bigger than any problem, big or small. Sometimes

He will use the dumbest thing to confuse the enemy while fixing the problem and bringing about an immediate answer or solution.

We sometimes face desperate circumstances or situations that can seem to overwhelm a person. I will agree that some problems can happen overnight like a pipe bursting suddenly, an accident, or a sickness. Those are sudden. An addiction problem, however, like the one I had for shopping, does not happen overnight. For some things to become an addiction, it has to repeatedly happen over time. This will become a habit, and believe it or not, it helps to shape a person's character and destiny. Mine is shopping; what is yours? Yours could be money, children, anger, spouse, smoking, drinking, drugs, sex, gossip, work, or anything else you might have gotten yourself into as an addiction. Anything that has you bound or you cannot control is an addiction.

You can overcome and become victorious. How do you get over an addiction? How do you get over a problem? First, you have to pray to God to help you identify the problem, get to the root cause of the problem, and then decide on the kind of achievement or result you desire and seek help. When you have done all that you can and it is not working, you have to give it to God. You have to be ready to do the right things that are required of you. You have to be willing to let go and let God and be willing to allow your mind to become free.

The Bible tells us that some things come only through prayer and fasting. Sometimes, however, the pain and hurt are so great that we find it difficult to be able to do either of these two things. Believe it or not, God will put someone in your life to fill in the gap and have these same people praying for you. He will have other people in place to help you to overcome.

Next, we have to be prepared to wait on the Lord. His timing is always perfect and on time. He is an on-time God. Other times we have to just give our way through. Give our money, give our time, and give our talent. Other times, we plain and simple have to just surrender.

A lot of the bad things we go through, we caused them ourselves based on prior actions and decisions. Other times, we go through stuff for our making. That stuff will cause some structure and balance to come into our lives, and in turn, this will help us form and shape our character and lead us into our destiny. Sometimes we go through it so that we can be a help to others who are facing similar problems or situations. After overcoming our challenges, it is easier for us to empathize or sympathize with others and not look down at them. We are able to speak life back into that person, letting him or her know not to be discouraged. Letting him or her know that he or she can live and will not die.

God will use anyone he chooses to get the work done. In the Bible, Judges 7:7, God used three hundred armed men from the army of thousands. The ones He chose were those who lapped like dogs while drinking water from the brook. They were the ones who won the battle for that nation. In the natural, it looked impossible, but in the spiritual, God gave them supernatural strength to do the work He called them to do. He was the one who chose those men. We are able to overcome our battle, the battle of the mind, because we are spiritually chosen and anointed by God.

God delivered people back then, and He is still delivering people now in our present time. We see the manifestation of this by the miracles that take place to the people around us.

Hope signifies trust, belief, and determination. Let me give you an example using the chicken and the egg to illustrate hope.

A chicken hatched an egg. It was "hatched," meaning this is now in the past, yesterday. What is inside the egg is the unknown, and it is supposed to be good. That represents victory, and it represents the future. The future is inside the shell of the egg and is unknown, and we hope and assume the future will be good. To get to what is inside the egg, we have to break the shell of the egg. The shell represents today. In other words, you have to break the shell of the egg today to get to what is inside the egg, which are victory and the future. So hope is seeing the future "victory" today based on yesterday's action.

God promised to make you victorious. Take hold of the promise. Isaiah 43:2 states, "When thou pass through the waters, I will be with thee; and through the rivers. They shall not overflow thee: when thou walkest through the fire, thou shall not be burned; neither shall the flame kindle upon thee."

So change your spiritual focus and give liberally to God's work. We must continue to pay our tithes and offerings. We must continue to read God's Word. We must continue to do this and do it in love. When we continue to give, this allows God's work to continue in the ministry. The doors of the church will remain open and obligations are met. Souls can continue to come into the Kingdom, and they can be saved, blessed, healed, delivered, and set free.

Do this with dedication and unto God. Do this joyfully and cheerfully and with an expectation from God. God will supernaturally intervene on your behalf and release His blessings and provisions in your life. Regardless of the crisis you are facing, do not be dismayed or discouraged. Focus on the will of God and your needs will be met.

GOD GOT THIS

In the Bible in the book of Esther, Esther was a Jewish orphan with no mother or father and was raised by her uncle Mordecai. She was from a position of obscurity. God, however, gave her favor, and she rose to her destiny and became queen of Persia. When the Jews' lives were threatened, Queen Esther, her uncle Mordecai, and all her Jewish people all over the country went on a three-day fast without food or water. She knew that she could receive the death penalty for appearing before the king without being summoned if he did not extend to her the golden scepter—she put her life on the line.

In Esther 5:15, God gave her favor in the king's eyes in that he not only stretched out his golden scepter toward her, but also he was willing to grant her request and bestow upon her up to half of his kingdom. God put her in the position of prominence and wealth and used her to save the Jewish people from destruction. God turned the battle around, and Haman was hanged on the very gallows that he prepared for Mordecai. The king allowed Mordecai to issue a decree that all Jews had the right to avenge themselves of their enemies. Mordecai was exalted and promoted to being the second-in-command to king Ahasuerus. The day that was meant for the Jews' destruction and great sorrow was turned into a day of victory.

Likewise, fast forward to our time. I read in the chain reference commentary section on page 599 of the Financial Freedom Bible by Morris Cerullo and also under www.Chick-fil-A.com where religious CEO S. Truett Cathy, founder and CEO of Chick-Fit-A company, the second largest chicken-based fast-food chain restaurant in the United States, has mandated that every Sunday, all his restaurants are to be closed to allow his staff time to worship. It is estimated that by closing his restaurant on Sundays, he loses about $500 million in income over the course of a year.

Concerning this, Cathy states, "Our decision to close on Sundays was our way of honoring God and directing our attention to things that are more important than business."

Because of his commitment to honor God by honoring the Sabbath, God blessed his business, and it is very successful. More than fifteen hundred restaurants generated in excess of $3.5 billion in annual sales in 2010, and it opened ninety new restaurants in 2011.

Cathy made another statement also: "I'd like to be remembered as one who kept my priorities in the right order. We live in a changing world, but we need to be reminded that the important things have not changed, and the important things will not change if we keep our priorities in their proper order."

Our priority in this world and especially in the church should be the things concerning God, which is to bring souls into the Kingdom of God and to spread his unadulterated and anointed Word. It is not about us. It is about Kingdom building. We can accomplish this as individuals and as a body when we come together and worship together. We are able to achieve this and more by fasting, praying, and reading God's Word daily. The result is an inflow of souls coming into the Kingdom.

In addition, we are required by God to give back to Him 10 percent of our time, 10 percent of our talent, and 10 percent of our tithes and a freewill offering back into His kingdom. The remaining 90 percent after tithes is taken out from our gross income is ours to keep.

Tithing will open the floodgates of God's blessings. If we are loyal to Him in what He has spoken and directed us to do, God promised in Malachi 3:10 to open the windows of heaven and pour out a blessing we will not have room enough to receive. We see this example played out when Solomon asked God only for wisdom, knowledge, and understanding on how to lead and rule God's people. We see how God blessed him more than he could imagine.

So let us focus and turn our attention to the things and business of God. Keep praying and bringing in your monies to the house of God. The church greatly appreciates it, and so does God. Like Solomon, God will do the same for you, and He will bless you.

God said to Solomon in I Kings 3:11–13, "Because thou hast ask this thing, and hast not asked for thyself long life: neither hast asked riches for thyself, nor hast asked the life of thine enemies: but hast asked for thyself understanding to discern judgement: Behold, I have done according to thy words: lo, I have given thee a wise and an understanding heart; so that there was none like thee before thee, neither after thee shall any rise like unto thee. And I have also given thee that which thou hast not asked, both riches, and honor: so that there shall not be any among the kings like unto thee all thy days."

Solomon was the richest and wisest man who ever lived. This should release your faith to believe that what God said, He will do.

GOD GOT THIS.

CONCLUSION

My goal here was to share with you why God requires us to pay tithes and offerings. It is also to make you aware that God requires us to present these gifts and offerings in a specific way.

God wants the best for each and every one of us. It is His wish that none should perish but have everlasting life. We can live a successful and healthy life if we follow His commandments and His rules here on earth, and God wants that for us.

We, however, have to set the standard and the bar high and maintain that standard. People will admire and respect you more for it. We should not strive to live a mediocre life. When you maintain that high level and standard, there are those who will admire you and will stand by you. There are those who will help to push you further into your destiny and will be happy to celebrate your accomplishments and achievements.

Do not be fooled. Not everyone will celebrate you and be there for you, especially when they see you appear to be moving up higher than they are in the world. The thing is, do not be moved by these people and the naysayers. Stand steadfast. Stand on God's Word. They do not know what you had to give up and what you had to go through to reach where you are today. They have no idea where God is taking you.

If you focus on God, the things of God, and His Kingdom, putting God first, He will withhold nothing good from you. He will put a hedge of protection around you. He will give you favor with people, places, and things. He will open doors for you that no one can close.

This is not to say you will never have to face difficulty in your lifetime. What I am trying to say is that when those times come around, and they will, He will be there to carry you through. He will make a way when it seems there is no way. An example of this in the Bible is Daniel, who was put in the lion's den with all those hungry lions. There is the story also of the three Hebrew boys who were thrown in the fire furnace. The hungry lions could not eat Daniel, and the three Hebrew boys did not smell of smoke when they were taken out the next day by the king himself. The people who were outside the fire furnace and came too close were badly burned by the fire, and some died. That shows how hot the fire was. The king said that when he looked in, he saw a fourth person in the fire with the three boys. That same day, the king declared that from that day onwards, everyone would worship the three Hebrew boys' God.

Continue to tithe your time, your talent, and your income to the church. It is good to give and sow into other ministries, but your tithes should be given to the place that you call your spiritual home and where you are spiritually fed. Just free up yourself and your mind to His will and let it go. If you do this, you will see the flow and the abundant blessings of God overtaking your life.

God said the greatest of His commandments is love. God said to love one another and ourselves as Christ loves the church. If this were done, the world would be a much better place.

Be encouraged and all is not lost. May God be in you and with you and may His grace and mercy forever be with you. I hope and pray that this book will be a blessing and encouragement to you as it was to me. I also hope that this book will have caused a few positive changes in your life and that you have a clearer picture and understanding about tithes and offerings.

May God rain His blessing of abundance on you.

SCRIPTURE REFERENCES

The Bible Scriptures (King James Version)

Blessing
Genesis 12:2
And I will make of thee a great nation, and I will bless thee, and make thy name great; and thou shall be a blessing.

Deuteronomy 1:11
The Lord God of your fathers make you a thousand time so many more as ye are and bless you, as he hath promised.

Curses
Malachi 3:9
Ye are cursed with a curse: for ye have robbed me, even this whole nation.

Creation
Ephesians 2:10
For we are his workmanship, created in Christ Jesus unto good works, which God hath before ordained that we should walk in them.

DEATH
Proverbs 18:21
Death and life are in the power of the tongue: and they that love it shall eat the fruit thereof.

GIVING AND RECEIVING
Proverbs 22:9
He that hath a bountiful eye shall be blessed; for he giveth of his bread to the poor.

Psalm 84:11
For the Lord God is a sun and shield: the Lord will give grace and glory: no good thing will he withhold from them that walk uprightly.

HONESTY
Proverbs 19:1
Better is the poor that walketh in his integrity, than he that is perverse in his lips, and is a fool.

HOPE
Romans 12:12
Rejoicing in hope: patient in tribulation; continuing instant in prayer.

INCREASES
Colossians 1:10
That ye might walk worthy of the Lord unto all pleasing, being fruitful in every good work, and increasing in the knowledge of God.

Money
1 Timothy 6:10
For the love of money is the root of all evil: which while some coveted after, they have erred from the faith, and pierced themselves through with many sorrows.

Poverty
Exodus 22:25–26
If thou lend money to any of my people that is poor by thee, thou shall not be to him as a usurer, neither shall thou lay upon him usury. If thou at all take thy neighbors' raiment to pledge, thou shall deliver it unto him by the sun goeth down.

Prayer
Proverbs 15:8
The sacrifice of the wicked is an abomination to the Lord: but the prayer of the upright is his delight.

Prosperity
Genesis 12:15–16
The prince also of Pharaoh saw her, and commended her before pharaoh: and the woman was taken into Pharaoh's house. And he entreated Abram well for her sake: and he had sheep, and oxen, and asses, and menservants and maidservants, and she asses, and camels.

Provision To The Poor
Psalm 140:12
Keep me, O Lord, from the hands of the wicked: preserve me from the violent man, who have purposed to overthrow my goings.

Sacrifices
Leviticus 3:1
And if his oblation be a sacrifice of peace offering, if he offer it of the herd; whether it be a male or female, he shall offer it without blemish before the Lord.

Tithes
Malachi 3:3–4
And he shall sit as a refiner and purifier of silver: and he shall purify the sons of Levi, and purge them as gold and silver, that they may offer unto the Lord an offering in righteousness. Then shall the offering of Judah and Jerusalem be pleasant unto the Lord, as in the days of old, and as in former years.

Vows
Genesis 28:20–21
And Jacob vowed a vow, saying, if God be with me, and will keep me in this way that I go, and will give me bread to eat, and raiment to put on, So that I come again to my father's house in peace; then shall the Lord be my God.

Wealth
Genesis 30:43
And the man increased exceedingly, and had much cattle, and maidservants, and menservants, and camels, and asses.

ACKNOWLEDGMENT

I WANT TO FIRST GIVE honor and thanks to God who is the head of my life and who has entrusted me to write this book on tithes and offerings.

My family who has supported me wholeheartedly. My husband, Joseph St. Marthe, who gave me the space I needed to pursue my goals. My two children, Clarence Dick and Anna-Kay Dick. I am a proud parent to see how you have embraced life, hold your heads up high, and have been a success in your choices in life. I know without a shadow of a doubt that God has more great gifts and blessings stored up for you. Keep up the good work. Love you all dearly.

To my great pastors, Apostle Scotto White and my late Apostle Cassandra White. Thanks for hearing God speak to you, thus allowing me to teach on the topic of tithes and offerings. God has used this beginning to start me out on this new journey, which has ultimately enabled me to write my first book on tithes and offerings.

Dr. Kim Ladson, you have been so patient and dedicated in mentoring and giving me your feedback on how to put my book together. From the very first day of our meeting, you saw this book.

To all those people whom I have not mentioned by name because space would not allow me, I just want to say a big thank you. Thank you for whatever input or part you played in this book.

BIBLIOGRAPHY

Cerullo, Morris. *Morris Cerullo Financial Freedom Bible*. P.O. Box 85277, San Diego, California 92186-5277, World Evangelism, 2012.

Dictionary.com. Accessed June 21, 2017. Dictionary.com.

Murdock, Mike. *Secrets of the Richest Man Who Ever Lived*. Petaling Jaya, Malaysia: Advantage Quest Publications, 2000.

AVERIL BURKE-ST. MARTHE HAS SERVED as a missionary in Jamaica, the West Indies, and the United States for over twenty years. She has also been ordained as a deaconess at her church.